Grandma Myrtle and her Helpers

© 2020 by TGS International, a wholly owned subsidiary of Christian Aid Ministries, Berlin, Ohio.

All rights reserved. No part of this book may be used, reproduced, or stored in any retrieval system, in any form or by any means, electronic or mechanical, without written permission from the publisher except for brief quotations embodied in critical articles and reviews.

ISBN: 978-1-950791-01-9

Cover and text layout design: Kristi Yoder

Cover art and illustrations in layout: Anton T. Leppo

Printed in the USA

Published by:

TGS International
P.O. Box 355
Berlin, Ohio 44610 USA
Phone: 330.893.4828
Fax: 330.893.2305
www.tgsinternational.com

Grandma Myrtle and her Helpers

Sylvia Yoder

Grandpa Chester and Grandma Myrtle
40 years together, in sickness and in health

Dedication

To my mother, Grandma Myrtle, with love.

Acknowledgments

- Thank you to the TGS editing staff for smoothing out the wrinkles in the story.
- Thanks to my siblings and their children who are living the same story with us. You are a wonderful team to work with.
- A special acknowledgment to my father, Chester Petre, who is "Grandpa" in this book. You have left a priceless example of commitment, in health and in sickness, to your children and grandchildren.

—Sylvia Yoder

Table of Contents

    Introduction 11
1. Hands and Feet for Grandma Myrtle 15
2. A Bag for a Bladder 23
3. Betty Washes Feet 31
4. Grandma Enjoys the Animals 35
5. What the Doctors Found 43
6. A Day at the Hospital... 49
7. Factory Teeth 55
8. A Fluffy Brown Pomeranian 61
9. Peanut and Prayers... 67
10. A Snowman for Grandma 73
11. Patience and Play Dough. 79
12. Spray Bottles and Shopping 87
13. Minnows and Whales 95
14. Shower Time.. 103
15. Choosing Willingness.. 111
16. A New Body—Someday... 117
    About the Author.. 121

Introduction

Hello, boys and girls. What do you like to do with your grandma? Bake cookies? Go for walks in the woods? Does she give you swing rides? Or take you shopping? In many ways the children in this book are just like you. They enjoy doing things with their grandma.

But the Yoders' grandma, Myrtle Petre, cannot do many things for herself, or for others. Her grandchildren have never seen Grandma stand or walk. They can hardly imagine that she used to drive or that long ago when she was a girl she could run and jump and play. But there are still things Grandma *can* do for her grandchildren. She can pray for them and read to them. She embroiders beautiful handkerchiefs and wall hangings for their birthdays.

Because Grandma Myrtle is handicapped, the Yoder children do many things for her that other children don't need to do for their grandparents. As you read their story, maybe you will find ideas of things you can do for your grandma to surprise her. Even if your grandma can walk, she might be happy to have a cold drink or to have her feet rubbed.

Grandma Myrtle has Multiple Sclerosis, or MS, a disease that damages the nerves. Our immune systems usually fight off germs to keep us from getting sick. But Grandma's immune system actually harms her body. MS eats away at the protective covering around her nerves. As her nerves become damaged, they cannot send messages of communication between her brain, her spinal cord, and other parts of her body. Slowly her nerves stop telling her muscles to move and different parts of her body become handicapped.

There is no cure for MS. Sometimes medicine will help, but someone with MS never gets better unless God performs a miracle. God has not chosen to heal Grandma Myrtle here on this earth.

MS is not contagious, which means it is not like chicken pox. If you play with someone who has chicken pox, you might get them too. You cannot get MS from someone else. But chicken pox go away in several days and you get better. MS does not go away.

God has made our bodies in wonderful ways. We don't often think about how our nerves get messages from our brain and send messages to our muscles so we can walk, wash dishes, mow the yard, or ride a bike. But every day, the parts of our bodies work together doing the jobs that God created them to do. We should often thank God for our health and pray for those who are handicapped and those who care for them.

—Sylvia Yoder

CHAPTER 1

Hands and Feet for Grandma Myrtle

The door into Grandma's living room burst open, and Jeneva and Jolynn trooped in from school. They shook off their jackets and kicked off their shoes as if trying to shed the chilly dampness of the October day. Grandma's house felt warm and cozy.

The girls bounced over to the couch where Grandma sat. "Good afternoon," Grandma greeted them. "Did you have a good day at school?"

Jolynn shrugged and brushed back the blond hair that always tickled her forehead. "We are learning about borrowing when we subtract. It's not fun."

Jeneva only stared at the bare windows and the

disheveled living room. "Are you tearing this place apart?" she asked Mama who was working in the kitchen.

"I'm cleaning Grandma's—" Mama began.

"I'm hungry," Jolynn interrupted. "What do I smell?"

"Pumpkin pie," Mama answered as she pulled a cookie sheet from the oven. "I'm making pies for Daddy and Grandpa. I had extra crust so I baked it for you girls." She set the sheet of crispy, hot strips on the table. "Save a few for Grandma."

"Yum!" the girls chorused as they heaped their plates and shook salt over the crispy strips. Jolynn placed some on a plate for Grandma, and Jeneva poured a sipper cup of Kool-Aid. They carried the cup and plate to the couch where Grandma could reach them.

"My living room is getting housecleaned today," Grandma said in answer to Jeneva's earlier question. "You girls are just in time to help your mama finish up."

Jeneva noticed the living room was rearranged. Grandpa's recliner was in the corner beside the toy box. The chime clock sat on a shelf above the chair. A little motto hung below the shelf. It said, "I might not be rich or famous, but I have priceless grandchildren." Mama had given it to Grandpa for his birthday when he turned fifty-five. Grandpa had smiled when he opened it. "That's the truth," he had exclaimed in his loud, jolly voice.

When Grandpa read stories to them, his loud voice

"Save a few for Grandma."

could make the scary parts scarier and the exciting parts more exciting. *If a stranger would talk to me in such a loud voice I would be frightened,* Jeneva thought. *But not Grandpa. All of us know how much he loves us.*

Grandma's weak voice broke into Jeneva's thoughts. "How was school today?"

"Oh, it was great," Jeneva said. "At recess it was raining so we played hide and seek upstairs. Whoever was 'it' had to use a mirror to find us."

"I never heard of playing hide and seek that way," Grandma said.

Jeneva was still thinking about voices. "Grandma, why is your voice so weak?" she asked.

"It's because of my MS. The muscles in my throat are weak, just like the muscles in the rest of my body. That is why I choke easily and can't cough very well when I have a cold."

"Oh," said Jolynn. Wanting to change the subject, she looked around the living room. "Hey, it looks different but nice in here. But why does your couch always stay in the same place, Grandma?"

"I like it here," Grandma answered.

Grandma spent most of her days on the couch. If the couch stayed in this spot, Grandma could look out the big doors and see who drove past. She could also watch the birds at the feeder in front of the window. And the couch was close enough to the table that she could still feel included during mealtime conversations.

"I wouldn't like to sit in one place all day," Jolynn said.

"No, you sure wouldn't," Grandma agreed. "You have always been a busy little lady. Even when you were a baby you didn't like to sit in one place very long. You would fuss and cry for your mama to carry you around. Finally you learned to walk. Then you were happier."

"Do you remember when I was a baby?" Jolynn's blue-gray eyes widened.

"Sure, I do. Your mama came to take care of me back then too. I can't do a lot of things that other grandmas do, but I get to watch my grandchildren grow because they come with their mamas to help me."

"I wouldn't mind sitting in one place for a whole day if I had a pile of books to read," Jeneva said.

"Reading would get old if you did it day after day," Grandma assured her.

Jeneva thought about that. *If I couldn't walk, I wouldn't be able to get a drink for myself when I'm thirsty. Someone would have to help me to the bathroom. I couldn't get a snack. I guess I wouldn't like that after all.*

"I don't like to read," Jolynn said.

"Maybe you will like it better when it's easier for you. You are only in second grade. It will go better when you have more practice," Grandma encouraged.

"I could sure read better than her when I was in second grade," Jeneva said.

"Well, you are good with your mind, and Jolynn is good with her hands," Mama said. "She writes more neatly in second grade than you do in fourth grade."

Jeneva became quiet at Mama's reprimand.

"What can we do?" the girls wondered when their snack was finished.

"Jeneva, would you go upstairs and tidy up where the little ones were playing today? And Jolynn, you can empty the dishwasher. I'll hang the curtains and start cooking supper," Mama planned.

A while later Jeneva called from the top of the stairs, "I'm finished. Now what shall I do?"

"I'd like to send one of my friends a birthday card," Grandma said, straining to make her voice heard. "Could you bring some cards from the dresser drawer in the green room?"

"Sure," Jeneva replied. Soon she came slowly down the steps, a book in one hand and card boxes in the other. She plopped the stack of card boxes onto Grandma's couch and curled up in a nearby chair to read. Then she looked up at Grandma.

Grandma was fumbling with the lid on the top box. *Plunk*, the box slipped to the floor. When the weather was damp and dreary like it was today, Grandma's hands worked even slower.

Jeneva put her book down and picked up the box of cards. "I'll help you," she offered. She showed the cards to Grandma and read the verses aloud.

"That's a good one," Grandma pointed at a beautiful flowery card after they had gone through several boxes. "I choose that one."

Jeneva laid the card and envelope on Grandma's lap and carried the stack of card boxes back upstairs.

Jolynn had come to join her older sister and stood beside the couch looking at Grandma's card. "Could you please go look in Grandpa's desk drawer?" Grandma asked her. "He has some money in a little black pouch. I would like a five-dollar bill to send along with this card."

Jolynn was surprised. *How does Grandma know where things are? She can't even walk! Maybe God helps her somehow*, she decided. She soon returned with the money. "Shall I write in the card for you?" she asked.

"Yes, I'd be glad if you would. You have such neat handwriting." Grandma gave Jolynn a special smile. "Here is a verse I want written for my friend." Grandma pointed to a verse in her Bible: "In all thy ways acknowledge him, and he shall direct thy paths."

Jolynn carried the card and the Bible to the kitchen table. Pushing her silky blond hair back from her face, she carefully printed the verse and the other words Grandma told her to write. When she was finished, she brought the card to Grandma.

"This looks very nice," Grandma approved. "Thank you, girls, for helping me with my card. What would I do without you to run little errands for me?"

"You don't have to worry about that, Grandma," Jeneva told her, "because you have us."

"Yes, God has blessed me with precious grandchildren," Grandma said with a smile.

CHAPTER 2

A Bag for a Bladder

Jeneva knocked lightly on the restroom door at church.

"Come in," Grandma greeted.

The first thing Jeneva noticed was Grandma's dress. "Grandma," she exclaimed, "we match today!"

"Well, we sure do," Grandma chuckled.

"Mama, did you know it?" asked Jeneva.

"No, I had no idea what dress Grandpa would put on Grandma this morning," Mama said.

Every Sunday morning Grandpa dressed Grandma Myrtle and brought her to church. When they arrived he pushed her wheelchair to the restroom. Then Mama or one of the other ladies arranged her hair. Grandpa declared his fingers were too big to manage Grandma's barrettes and the pins in her head covering.

"May I push Grandma out to her bench?" Jeneva asked. She opened the door as Mama finished pinning Grandma's covering.

"Sure." Mama put the comb in the cupboard out of sight from all the church ladies who would use the restroom that day.

Carefully Jeneva pushed the wheelchair around the corner to the short bench where there was a spot for Grandma's wheelchair.

"I want to sit on Grandma's bench," Jolynn whispered as she followed Mama into the auditorium.

"Okay, go sit down. Grandpa is holding Baby Betty. I need to get her," Mama replied.

Grandma reached for the blanket-wrapped baby as Mama squeezed past her chair. Mama snuggled Baby Betty in the crook of Grandma's arm. Grandma could hold little babies like Betty, but when they got big enough to be wiggly they could slide off her lap.

During the service Melissa Jones was sitting behind them. Soon after the opening devotional, she tapped Mama's shoulder and whispered in her ear. Mama handed Betty to Melissa, then leaned forward and whispered to Aunt Edith.

"Girls, go sit with Daddy," Mama whispered. "I need

Grandma Myrtle holding Baby Betty.

to take Grandma home." Mama pushed Grandma's chair to the entrance, while Aunt Edith hurried to the basement. She returned carrying a bucket of soapy water and a rag to mop up the puddle on the floor where the wheelchair had been parked.

The service was almost over when Mama returned, but Grandma was not with her.

"What happened this morning?" Daddy asked as they drove home.

"Grandma's bladder is getting so weak," Mama answered. "She didn't realize anything was going on until it was too late. By then there was a puddle under her."

"Why is Grandma like that?" Jolynn asked.

Mama thought a little. "The nerves in Grandma's body don't tell her muscles what to do as they used to. Her body is getting weaker, including the nerves that let her know she needs to use the restroom. I think I need to talk to her doctor about it."

During the next several weeks, Grandma had appointments with her family doctor and with a specialist in the big city of Columbus. The specialist said Grandma Myrtle would need to have surgery.

Then one evening Mama announced, "Girls, tomorrow you will stay with Grandpa and Mommi Yoder at their house after school. I'm going to the hospital with Grandpa and Grandma. If Grandma Myrtle feels well enough after surgery, you can visit her in the hospital tomorrow evening."

"When can she come home?" Jolynn wondered.

"It depends how well she recovers," Mama replied. "But hopefully in two weeks or less."

It was several evenings later when Daddy drove them to Columbus. Going to the big hospital was exciting and scary. But Daddy knew where to park and led them across the walkway to the entrance. A big sign read, "Welcome to Riverside Methodist Hospital."

When Brandon saw the elevator doors, he cheered. "We get to ride on a alligator!"

"It's an *elevator*," Jolynn corrected.

"That's all right, son." Mama patted Brandon's head. "Jolynn used to say 'unkfunk' for elephant when she was little." Mama's eyes twinkled at Jolynn as the family entered the elevator.

Jeneva was standing next to the buttons by the elevator doors. "Push number seven," Daddy told her as the doors slid shut. "Grandma is on the seventh floor."

Grandma was sleeping when they walked into her room. She lay still and pale under the white sheets. A big piece of tape covered a tube in her neck, and IV lines were hooked to her. She opened her eyes and smiled when she heard the children. She tried to lick her dry lips, and Mama gave her an ice chip from the cup on the stand beside her bed.

"Hi, Grandma," the children greeted.

"Can we see where Grandma's tummy was cut?" Jeneva wondered.

Mama's eyes met Grandma's. "I don't mind," Grandma said, so Mama lifted the sheet and pointed to a strange-looking spot on Grandma's tummy.

"This little hole is called a stoma. The doctor took Grandma's bladder out and made this little hole. He took a piece of her intestine and fastened it to her kidneys. Now Grandma doesn't have a bladder anymore. Instead she has a bag that sticks to her tummy. It's sticky on the back and fastens to the skin around her stoma. We can turn this little valve on the bottom of the bag to empty it when it's full."

"That means no more puddles," Jeneva said as she patted Grandma's arm.

"That's right," Grandma agreed. "And I'll be thankful about that."

"Does your tummy hurt, Grandma?" Jolynn wondered.

"The tube in my neck hurts worse than the cut on my stomach," Grandma replied.

"Why do you need that tube?" Jolynn asked.

"Grandma's blood veins are small and hard to find," Mama explained. "So the doctor put this line in the big vein in her neck. Now the nurses don't have to poke

Grandma as often to give her medicine or draw blood for tests."

In a few days Grandma Myrtle was back home on her own couch. Once a week Mama changed Grandma's bag, carefully washing the skin around the stoma with special soap. She measured the stoma and cut a hole in the bag so that it would fit just right. A ring of putty around the hole protected Grandma's skin from moisture. The sticky part of the bag stuck to Grandma's tummy.

As Jeneva watched, she thought of all the people who needed to use bags like Grandma did. Someone must have worked a long time to figure out how to make a stoma and a bag that would stay attached to a stomach.

"This is a blessing compared to how things used to be," Grandma rejoiced. "I'm thankful for all the 'friends' I have that make my life easier. I have a wheelchair for my legs—and now a bag for my bladder!"

CHAPTER 3

Betty Washes Feet

Mama stood at Grandma's kitchen sink, chopping juicy red tomatoes. Grandpa had picked a big white bucket of tomatoes that morning and Mama was canning tomato soup for Grandpa and Grandma to eat next winter. There was nothing Grandpa liked better on a cold evening than crunchy toasted cheese sandwiches and tomato soup.

Little Betty opened the cupboard door and pulled on a stack of basins and bowls. "Wash, wash," she said, looking at Mama. By now, Betty was old enough to walk and say a few words, but sometimes it was hard for the family to understand her.

"Don't dig in Grandma's cupboards," Mama said. "Come help me wash tomatoes."

Betty shook her head. "Wash Grandma."

"Grandma can't wash tomatoes," Mama said. She dried her hands and went to Betty. Then she laughed. Betty was pulling on the purple basin Jolynn used when she washed Grandma's feet.

"I wash feet," Betty insisted. Her big eyes looked up at Mama.

Mama patted Betty's head. "Do you want to wash Grandma's feet?"

"Yes! I wash!" Betty hopped up and down, pleased that Mama understood.

"Not right now," Mama told her. "You will make a big mess. Wait until Jolynn gets back from school. She will help you."

Mama shut the cupboard door and carried Betty into the living room. She sat on the couch beside Grandma. "I couldn't understand what Betty wanted to do until I saw she was trying to get the purple basin."

Betty slid off Mama's lap and got a bottle of lotion out of the basket on the end of the couch.

"Grandma, lotion?"

"Yes, you can lotion my feet," Grandma said.

Betty sat on the floor and squirted a big glob of lotion on each of Grandma's feet. Lotion plopped onto the floor

"I wash feet."

while Betty smeared it over Grandma's feet and legs.

"I'll clean you up when she's done." Mama assured Grandma.

"I don't mind the mess." Grandma chuckled.

When Jolynn came in the door from school that afternoon, Betty ran to meet her. "Wash. I wash," she said as she opened the cupboard door and tugged on the purple basin. "I can't, Lynn. Help!"

Jolynn laughed. "Mama, she wants to wash Grandma's feet. How does she remember that?"

"This morning she fussed until I understood what she wanted. I was busy and said you would help her. She has been waiting for you."

As soon as Jolynn finished her snack, she spread a towel on the floor under Grandma's feet and filled the purple basin with warm, soapy water. Betty got a wash cloth and together they washed and dried Grandma's feet. They rubbed in more lotion and slipped on fresh socks.

"Thank you, girls," Grandma said when they were finished. "My feet feel fresh. It's special to have such good little nurses." Betty crawled up to sit beside Grandma and smiled.

CHAPTER 4

Grandma Enjoys the Animals

The Yoders had just come home from church. They paused on the porch while Daddy unlocked the front door.

"Is anyone coming for dinner?" Jolynn asked hopefully.

Often when they asked that question Mama would tease them. "Yes, the Yoder family."

She liked to hear them say, "Mama, we mean company!"

Today Mama said, "Grandpa and Grandma are coming."

"Oh, I will stay here and open the door when they come," Brandon announced.

"Are you trying to be a little gentleman?" Jolynn teased as she began setting the table.

Mama poured peas into a kettle, added water, and placed it on the burner. She opened the oven door and lifted the lid on the roast pan to check if it was done.

"Betty, come upstairs with me. I'll help you change your dress," Daddy called. They climbed the stairs, hand in hand.

"Grandpa and Grandma are here," Brandon announced. He opened the door while Grandpa bumped Grandma's wheelchair up the steps.

"You are a handsome little doorkeeper," Grandma praised.

Jolynn came from the kitchen. She looked up at Grandpa. "Can I push Grandma to the table?"

"Sure." Grandpa stepped away and Jolynn took over. She situated Grandma's chair so that the footrests did not bump the table legs. If that happened, Grandma couldn't reach her plate. Jolynn locked the brakes so the chair couldn't roll backward.

"Where is your apron, Grandma?" Jolynn wondered.

"Grandpa forgot to get it off the back of the couch. But you can get me a dish towel."

Jolynn tucked one end of a clean dish towel around the neck of Grandma's purple dress. She smoothed the other end over Grandma's lap.

"Thank you, Jolynn," Grandma said. "That will keep my Sunday dress clean."

The family gathered around the table. As they sang "Father, We Thank Thee," Jeneva listened to Grandpa's deep bass voice rumbling along.

While they were passing the bowls and dishing out food, Mama's cup tipped. Water rushed across the table and poured onto Grandpa's lap. "There's a flood!" he exclaimed, quickly pushing his chair back while Mama jumped up for a towel.

When the mess was cleaned up, Jolynn said, "I'm surprised that Mama's cup is the one that spilled."

"I am glad it didn't spill on Grandma, because she can't get out of the way," Brandon said.

"Grandpa sure moved fast," Daddy teased.

When everyone was finished eating and the table was cleared, Mama said, "Shall we push Grandma to the barn to see the chickens?"

"Yes, let's!" the children chorused as they ran for their jackets.

"Here, Grandma, you may use my favorite blanket," Jeneva said as she tucked the blanket under Grandma's legs. "I don't want you to get cold."

A merry group headed toward the barn. Jeneva and Jolynn helped each other push the wheelchair, and Brandon hurried ahead to move the bricks that were stacked under the gate. "Your chair can't get over these bricks," he told Grandma.

"The bricks are supposed to keep the baby goats from slipping under the gate," Mama explained.

Betty's pet goat saw the little procession coming toward the barn and bounded over to meet her human friends. "This is Rosie," Jeneva told Grandma.

Jolynn told Grandma the names of the other goats and the little Holstein calf.

Mama moved the wheelchair closer to the chicken house door. "Watch out for Rosie," Jeneva cautioned as Jolynn slid the door open. "She likes to sneak in and eat the chicken feed."

Grandma leaned forward to peer into the chicken house.

"Here, I'll bring you one to hold." Jeneva carried her special hen Josie outside and set her on Grandma's lap. Josie sat still while Grandma petted her.

"Let's show Grandma our little kid," Jolynn suggested. "He's in the back pen in the barn so he learns not to get out."

"Grandma's wheelchair will get manure on it if we push it into the barn," Mama cautioned. "But you can bring the kid out to show her."

Jeneva snapped the blue leash on the kid's collar. They laughed to see how he frisked and jumped like a pet puppy out for a walk. "He has to eat grass and feed now," Brandon told Grandma. "He doesn't get a bottle anymore." Then Brandon called for his pet calf,

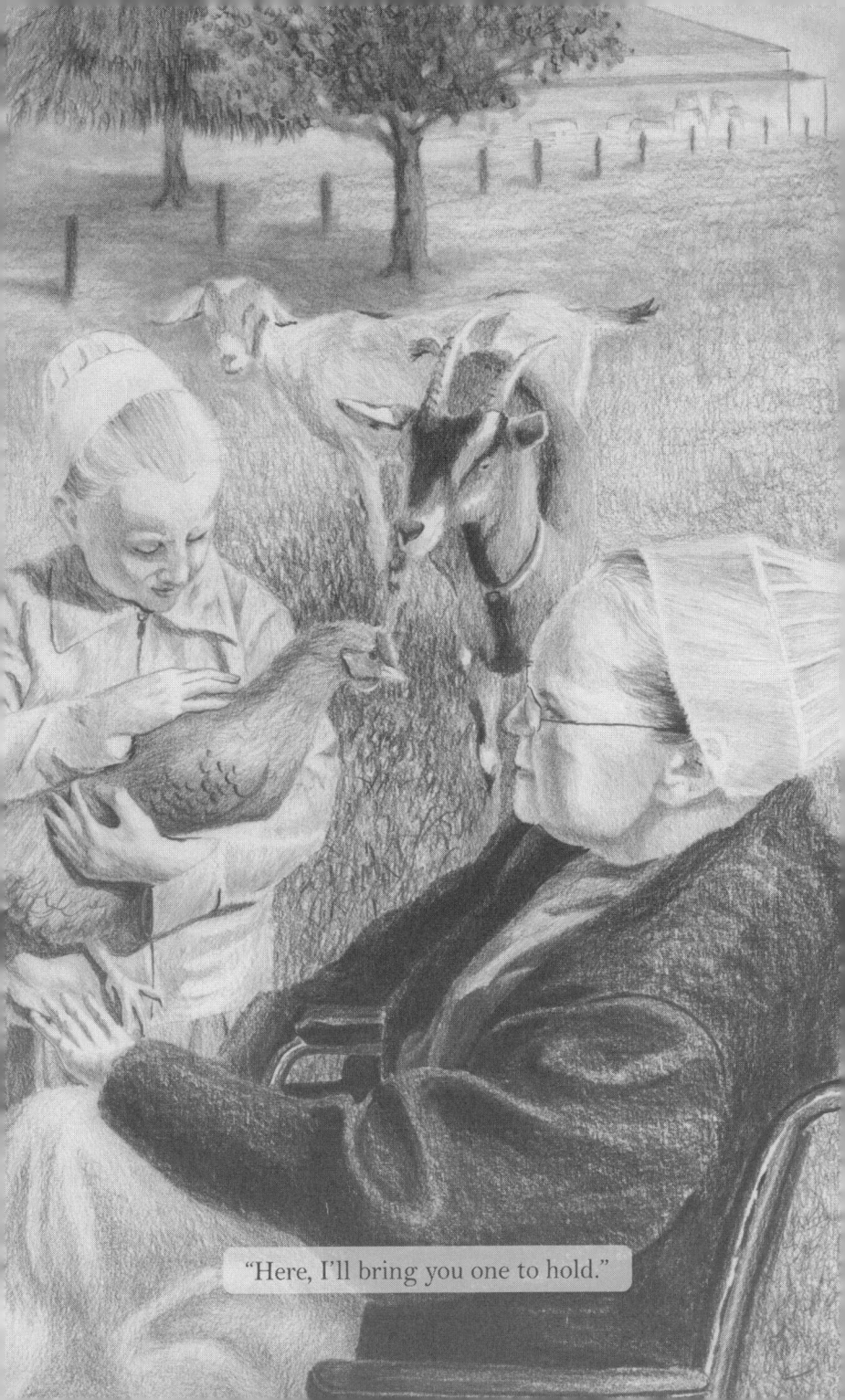

and Grandma laughed as he put his arm around the calf's neck and walked around the pasture.

Jolynn and Jeneva pushed Grandma's chair as they all headed back toward the house. "Thank you for showing me your little farm," Grandma said as her chair bounced over the yard.

"Careful," Mama cautioned her ambitious daughters. "If you push too fast, Grandma might fly out and Grandpa or Daddy will have to pick her up."

"I've had some wild rides in this chair," Grandma said. "One time when your mama was a young girl we went to a park for a picnic. Grandpa parked my wheelchair but forgot to lock the brakes. The others went on a walk and I sat in the shade to wait for them. Suddenly my wheelchair started rolling faster and faster down toward the river. My hands weren't strong enough to grab the wheels and stop myself. But then the chair turned a little and I crashed into a fence."

"Grandma!" Jeneva exclaimed. "Did you get hurt?"

"My knees were sore for a little while. Thankfully I didn't fly out of my chair and land in the water." Grandma laughed, then added, "My family was surprised to see me at the edge of the river."

"It's funny now," Mama said, "but it wasn't back then."

"Grandma, I didn't know you were already in a wheelchair when Mama was a girl," Jolynn said. "You haven't been able to walk for a long time."

"About twenty years," Grandma replied. "When I first found out I had MS, I could still walk, but my feet dragged. Then I could hardly lift my legs. When Aunt Edith was born I couldn't walk well enough to carry her, so your mama and your uncle Ben would bring her to my rocking chair. Then I used the wheelchair when I went away from home. Finally I was so crippled I needed it all the time."

"That story makes me sad," Jeneva said quietly.

"Sometimes I felt sad too," Grandma told her. "But God is good to me. He gave me a husband and five children who take good care of me."

"And now you have grandchildren to help you too," Mama added as the girls pushed Grandma's chair to the spot where Grandpa was waiting to load Grandma into the van.

"I hope you have enjoyed your tour of the Yoder family farm!" Jeneva said with a flourish, pretending to be a tour guide.

"I have," Grandma assured her. "Now I'll know what you are talking about when you tell me about your chores and animals. Thank you, children, for the interesting afternoon."

CHAPTER 5

What the Doctors Found

One wintry evening Mama called Jeneva and Jolynn into their bedroom. "I'm going to Columbus tomorrow with Grandma," she said as she showed them the clothes she had laid out for them.

"Will you be gone when we wake up? Who will comb our hair?" Jolynn worried.

"Yes, I'm leaving before you wake up. But Aunt Janice is coming. She will comb you and take Brandon and Betty home with her. They will stay with Mommi Yoder, and you will go there after school."

"May we walk on Mommi's road?" Jeneva asked eagerly.

"No!" Jolynn protested. "I'm scared of the dogs along

that road. Ever since that dog bit me last summer I'm scared of big dogs."

Mama thought a bit. "Just ride on the school van. I don't think you should walk if Jolynn is scared."

"Aww, those dogs wouldn't hurt a flea," Jeneva scoffed. "Scaredy-cat! All because you are scared, we can't walk."

"If a German shepherd would bite you, Jeneva, maybe you would change your mind. You are picking a fight, and I want you to be kind," Mama said.

Jeneva changed the subject. "Why is Grandma going to the doctor again?"

"Her stomach is swollen and miserable again so she's having a colonoscopy," Mama answered.

"What's that?" Jeneva forgot to be miffed about not walking to Mommi's. New words intrigued her and she had never heard this one before.

"From what I understand, the doctor puts a little camera inside of the person and takes pictures of their colon," Mama explained.

"Will it hurt as bad as a dog bite?" Jolynn asked. Big words didn't interest Jolynn. She was still thinking about big dogs.

Mama laughed.

"Grandma won't know what's happening because the doctor will give her medicine to put her to sleep."

The next morning it seemed strange with Mama gone.

Aunt Janice helped Daddy fix breakfast and combed the girls' hair. She helped Brandon and Betty get dressed.

That afternoon the girls reminded the school van driver to take them to Grandpa Yoder's house. When they drove past the place where the dogs lived, Jeneva was quiet. Jolynn was glad her sister didn't tell the other children how scared she was of dogs.

It was suppertime when Mama walked into Mommi Yoder's kitchen. Daddy had come to Grandpa's place after work. "How was your day?" he asked as Mama sat beside him.

"I guess it was alright," Mama said. "While Grandma had her colonoscopy I went to see Edith at the University Hospital." Edith's husband Ezra had cancer and needed to spend a lot of time in the hospital.

"How was Ezra?" Daddy asked.

"He has a cough that worries the doctor and he doesn't have an appetite," Mama said.

"How is Grandma?" Jeneva and Jolynn could hardly wait their turn to ask.

"She's tired. But I gave her a shower after we got home and she's resting on her couch." Mama swallowed a bite. "She has a large tumor in her colon. That's what is obstructing her bowels and making her so miserable." Mama paused to look around the table. "The doctor thinks she has cancer."

The family stared at Mama, faces stricken. The noise around the table stopped. "Is the doctor sure?" Grandpa Yoder asked.

"Well, no—not completely sure. We have to wait on the biopsy results—but from what he can see he thinks—it will be malignant," Mama said, her voice strained.

"What is malignant?" Jolynn asked.

"It means cancer," Mama said.

Jeneva and Jolynn were quiet as they helped clear the table and helped wash the dishes. The adults did not visit much either. When it was time to go home, Mama gathered up coats and back packs. "Thank you for keeping the children today," she told Mommi.

"Any time," Mommi Yoder assured her.

"I hope you all sleep well tonight," Grandpa said as he waved from the doorway.

The ride home was quiet too. It was hard to absorb such bad news. Cancer!

Later, Mama came to the girls' bedroom to say good night.

"Will Grandma die?" Jolynn asked.

"We don't know," Mama replied. "But she could get very sick."

"I can't believe our grandma has cancer," Jeneva said. Cancer was not a new word for her. Even Jolynn knew what it meant.

"I guess—I had a long day."

"Will her hair fall out—like Uncle Ezra's?" Jolynn asked next.

"It might if she has chemotherapy." Mama said.

"Poor Grandma," the girls said together.

"Let's say your prayers," Mama said. "You girls need to get to sleep."

But when Mama started to say their nighttime prayer, she burst into tears. Both girls hurried over and put their arms around her and they cried together.

"I guess—I had a long day," Mama said shakily. "And when you said, 'Poor Grandma,' I just couldn't bear to think of everything she might have to suffer. Let's try not to worry about it. God will take care of Grandma."

After prayer Mama went out to the living room where Daddy was rocking Betty. "I heard the girls," he said. "They would sure miss their grandma if she died."

"Yes, they would," Mama agreed. She sat down on the couch near Daddy. "We would all miss her." she added.

CHAPTER 6

A Day at the Hospital

Several weeks later Mama was gone again when the girls got up. Once again Aunt Janice came to help them. Grandma Myrtle was having surgery that day to remove the tumor from her colon.

When Daddy prayed at the breakfast table, he asked God to bless Mama, to guide the doctor's hands during surgery, and to heal Grandma according to His will. After the girls left for school, Daddy drove to Columbus to be with Mama while Grandma was in surgery.

The school day dragged by so slowly, but that evening there was good news. The doctor had been able to remove the entire tumor, and the cancer was contained.

All the cancer was inside the tumor and none had spread to other parts of Grandma's body.

"The doctor did a colostomy," Mama told them. "He made a stoma on the other side of Grandma's stomach. Now she will have two bags."

Mama paused and looked at Jolynn and Jeneva. "On Saturday I plan to spend the day with Grandma at the hospital and you girls can go with me." Jolynn clapped her hands and Jeneva gave an excited little hop.

Early Saturday morning the whole family scurried about, getting ready to leave. Daddy and Brandon were going to a home and garden show in Columbus, and they would drop off Mama, Jeneva, and Jolynn at the hospital. Little Betty would spend the day with Mommi Yoder.

Betty was not happy with this arrangement. At Grandpa Yoder's house, she cried and clung to Mama. "I want to go to see Grandma!" she wailed.

"Not this time, dear," Mama told her. "The hospital is not a place for a girlie your size to spend the day." Mommi Yoder took Betty and tried to distract her with a cookie while Mama slipped quietly out the door.

It took one hour to drive to Riverside Hospital in Columbus. Just before arriving, they drove past the University Hospital where Uncle Ezra had stayed. *What a huge hospital*, Jeneva thought as they drove past. *I'm so glad Ez and Edith aren't there anymore. I'm glad they can be at home with their little girlies*.

"Have a good day. I'll see you about four o'clock," Daddy said as he left them at the hospital entrance.

The girls were glad Mama was along to guide them to Grandma's room on the eleventh floor. Grandma was in bed and had an IV port in her neck, but she was awake and a friendly nurse was feeding her breakfast.

"Good morning, Grandma," they said.

"This is a surprise!" Grandma exclaimed. "I'm glad you came with your mama for the day."

At first it was exciting to look out the big window from so high up. Construction workers were adding another part onto the hospital, and the girls watched the big crane lift pieces of steel up to the workers who were setting them in place for walls.

Grandma's bed had buttons that made it go up and down, and they gave Grandma several rides. The Germ-X dispenser was touchless. All they had to do was hold their hands under it and out came Germ-X. The girls used Germ-X until Mama told them to stop.

Time dragged. "I'm hungry," Jolynn announced about mid-morning.

"Can we go to the cafeteria?" Jeneva begged.

Mama laughed. "I'm guessing you are bored, not hungry. But yes, I suppose we could go get a snack."

It was fun to choose a snack and plan what they would

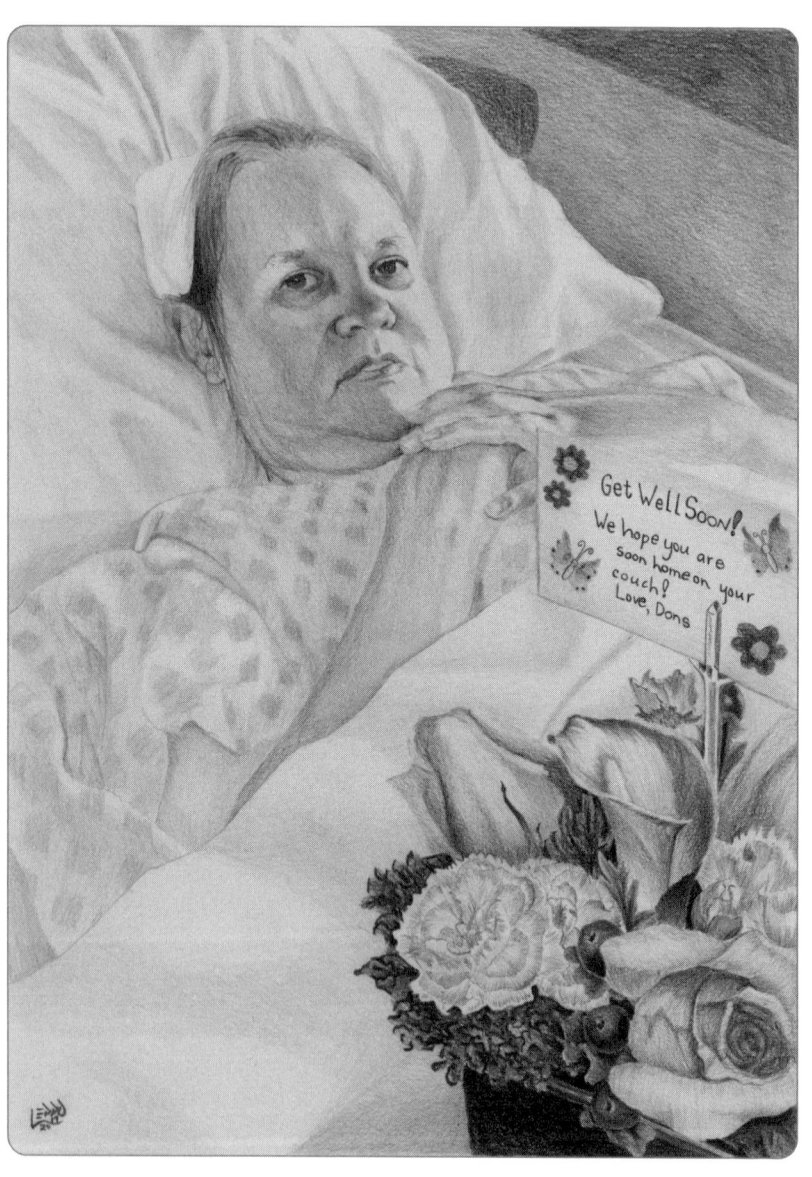

"I'm glad you came with your mama for the day."

buy for lunch. The food looked so good.

At lunch time Mama spooned warm broth into Grandma's mouth. The girls didn't think Grandma's lunch looked nearly as good as the food they had bought in the cafeteria. But Grandma said it tasted good to her after Mama added some salt.

By two o'clock the girls were ready to go home. "Could we have another snack?" Jeneva wondered.

Mama put down her hand sewing and looked in her wallet. "I had twenty dollars this morning and there are a few dollars left. I guess you girls can eat until my money is gone."

This time the girls knew the way to the cafeteria. They bought little bags of chips, a bottle of juice, and a bottle of water for Mama. There were only a few coins left.

Daddy and Brandon arrived just before four o'clock. "Look, Grandma," Brandon said, showing her the bag of candy and a stuffed lamb he had gotten at the show.

Mama and the girls began to gather their things. Grandpa was coming to the hospital to be with Grandma Myrtle, and Mama called to ask when he would arrive. "I'll be fine until he gets here," Grandma said. "Just go home. Little Betty will be glad to see you."

As they left the hospital, Daddy told them to watch for Grandpa's vehicle on the other side of the interstate. Twenty minutes later Brandon spotted a black

Ford minivan blinking its lights. It was Grandpa, and they all waved eagerly.

At Mommi Yoder's, Betty came running. She leaped into Mama's arms and Mama snuggled her close. "She missed her family today," Mommi said.

A tired but happy family gathered around the supper table at home. It had been an interesting day but it was good to be at home together again.

CHAPTER 7

Factory Teeth

Brandon opened the door to Grandpa's mechanic shop. He listened, hoping to hear Grandpa whistling or banging somewhere. All was quiet. Next he looked out the office window. Grandpa's dump truck was not parked outside the shop. *I wish we would have got here sooner, then I could have gone with Grandpa today.* Brandon trudged back to the house.

Betty was bringing all the dolls and teddy bears from the play room. She wanted to set up a train. Brandon pulled the kitchen chairs into the living room and set them in a row. He found all the footstools and set dolls and bears on them, too. Then he climbed on the engine and Betty sat in the caboose.

"Come, Brandon and Betty," Mama called. "Grandma's sewing machine doesn't work so I need to take some mending home."

It did not take Mama long to do the mending, and they headed back to Grandma's house. "The school house, the school house," the children chanted as they passed the school where Jeneva and Jolynn attended.

As Grandma's house came into view, Brandon's chant stopped. He bounced as wildly as his booster seat allowed. "The dump truck, Grandpa's dump truck! He's home for lunch. Mama, can I ride with him after lunch?"

"You have to ask him," Mama said as she parked beside the big truck in the driveway. Brandon's door flew open and Mama watched a streak shooting toward the house.

Grandpa had found leftovers in the fridge and was sitting at the table eating lunch. He and Brandon were discussing the dump truck ride when Mama and Betty came in.

"I want to go too," Betty pleaded.

"No, Betty. You are too little. You are only three. When you turn four like me you can go." Brandon's chest puffed with importance. "Or maybe when I'm six and go to school you can have turns."

"But I want to go!" Betty wailed.

"You can stay here and be my good helper. Sit on the

other side of Grandpa and eat your lunch," Mama said as she set more plates on the table.

"Pizza!" the children cheered. Mama snipped another piece of pizza with the kitchen shears. She was fixing a plate for Grandma. Next she filled a sipper cup and carried Grandma's lunch to her.

"Why did you give Grandma a sipper cup?" Betty asked.

"Her hands are weak and can't hold a cup very well without spilling it," Mama replied. She put a cushion under Grandma's arm and helped her sit up a little straighter. Then she set the plate and cup where Grandma could reach them.

"I'm done!" Brandon announced.

Mama looked at Brandon's empty plate. "How can you be done already? You wolfed that lunch!"

Grandpa was laughing. "He's not going to miss his ride."

"I need a drink to take with me." That was Brandon's next concern. Mama handed him a sipper cup. Brandon stopped in front of the couch on his way to the door. Grandma had taken only a few bites of pizza. "Why do you eat so slowly?" he asked.

"Because my teeth aren't as sharp as yours," Grandma told him.

Brandon clicked his teeth together. "Why not?"

Grandma's mouth was full so Mama answered. "God

"If you're going with me, you'd better come."

made your teeth, Brandon, but Grandma's teeth were made in a factory." Now Brandon really looked puzzled. Mama looked amused. "The teeth God gave Grandma got weak and started to break, so the dentist pulled them all out," she explained. "Now she has false teeth. They work, but they aren't as good as the teeth God makes."

"They sure aren't," Grandma agreed.

"Can I see your teeth?" Brandon wondered.

"No," Mama answered. "Grandma is trying to eat right now."

By this time Grandpa had finished his lunch. "If you're going with me you better come," he told Brandon.

Betty scurried along outside and Mama followed. Betty had clambered up the high steps into the truck before Mama was off the porch.

"Betty, get down. You can't go," Brandon told her. "Mama, come get her!" he called.

Mama reached up and lifted Betty to the ground. "Come help Mama. There are washcloths you can fold."

Back in the house, Betty's little hands flew. Grandma's washcloths were more fun to fold than the ones at home. Betty sang at the top of her voice, "I'll sly away, oh glory, I'll sly away in the morning. When I die, hallelujah by and by, I'll sly away."

"I like to hear how she says *s* instead of *f*," Grandma said quietly when Mama helped her lie down to rest.

"Do you like me to sing to you?" Betty asked a bit later.

"Sure," Grandma answered. "Can you sing, 'Jesus Loves Me'?"

After a few rounds of that Betty asked, "Shall I sing, 'All God's Creatures'?"

"Oh yes, I like that song," Grandma assured her. Soon a tottery stack of washcloths stood on the table. Grandma was sound asleep, and Betty dashed off to play with her doll.

CHAPTER 8

A Fluffy Brown Pomeranian

Four children bounced around Mama. "Daddy has a building to move. May we go with him?"

Mama looked up from the rose bush she was pruning. "That's not my decision," she said. "Go ask Daddy."

Daddy was hooking the trailer to his truck. He looked up to see a mini stampede heading his way.

"Daddy, Daddy, may we go with you?"

Daddy thought a little. "Yes, but you can't go barefoot. Get something on your feet and bring Betty's car seat."

With a flurry of activity and a banging of doors, the Yoder children were soon ready to go.

If the four children had realized they were about to

find an answer to their prayers, they would have been even more excited. All summer they had been begging for a dog. Their last dog had been very naughty. No amount of discipline and training could change his ways. He barked at strangers, chased vehicles, and ran away. Over and over Mama said, "He's nothing but a waste of money." One day he met his end under the rear wheels of a vehicle.

The children began talking about a new dog. Brandon wanted a big dog he could wrestle with. Jolynn was afraid of German Shepherds. She was glad when Daddy said, "No big dogs. They might scare customers away when they come to the shop to look at storage buildings."

Jeneva wanted a puppy she could train. But Mama said, "No more puppies. We don't want an untrained dog running around here, and I don't have time to help train a dog."

They simply could not find a dog that suited everyone, but they kept talking and hoping and praying the right one would turn up.

The building Daddy had to move that afternoon was part of an animal rescue shelter. The man at the shelter was friendly and showed the children some of his dogs. In one cage they spotted a fluffy, brown Pomeranian named Peanut. He was small, friendly, and already trained. He had lived with an elderly lady until she needed to go to a nursing home. Now he lived at the shelter, and he needed a new home.

The children talked about Peanut all the way home. Daddy would only say, "We have to talk to Mama."

The truck had barely stopped near the house before the doors burst open and the children jumped out.

"Mama, we found a dog!"

"His name is Peanut and he's already trained."

"Can we adopt him? Daddy said we have to ask you."

"Stop, stop!" Mama hushed the children. "I can't think when you all talk at once. We won't make any decisions until I talk to Daddy. Supper is ready. Sit down at the table. Daddy will soon be in from the shop."

The children sat, but they kept on talking. "Mama, you have to say yes. He has the sweetest face." Jeneva kept begging.

Daddy walked into the kitchen. "Sounds like you found a dog," Mama said.

"The children did," he replied wryly. "Where is Jolynn?"

Mama turned from the stove. "I don't know. I thought she was here."

"She's in the office," Jeneva said. "She went to call Grandma."

Mama laughed. "I'm not surprised."

Grandma was one person the children were allowed to call without asking permission. Day after day Grandma sat on her couch. She enjoyed when her grandchildren called to brighten her day with bits of news: a new baby goat, a nest of kittens, round bales rolling off the wagon at the end of the driveway. Grandma could never guess what she would hear next.

Soon Jolynn reappeared. After prayer Mama asked, "Is this dog trained? How old is he?" Finally she said, "I can't say what I think without seeing him."

. . . .

"No wonder you like Peanut so much," Mama said the next day at the shelter. "He looks like a nice dog for our family."

Daddy signed the papers and paid the shelter man. The fluffy, brown Pomeranian hopped into the truck for a ride to his new home. Peanut stank badly from living with so many other animals. Daddy opened all the windows for fresh air.

"We will bathe him, Daddy." Jeneva tried to defend her new pet.

"He needs a haircut. That will help too," Mama added.

When they got home Jeneva fixed food and water bowls for Peanut.

Jolynn hurried to the phone. "Grandma wants us to bring Peanut along next time we come to her house," she announced when she hung up.

"We can do that," Mama agreed. "And let's hope he smells better by then!"

Peanut hopped into the truck for a ride to his new home.

CHAPTER 9

Peanut and Prayers

Mama picked up her basket of supplies and turned off the lights. "Is everyone ready to go to Grandma's?"

"I still need to put Peanut on his leash," Jeneva called. When she led him to the van, Peanut hopped right in with the children and sat on the floor, whining a happy dog tune.

They soon arrived at Grandma's house. Grandma was sitting on the couch where Grandpa put her every morning. Her quiet house was cheered by a babble of excited children.

"Oh! He is cute." Grandma exclaimed when she saw Peanut. "Put him up on the couch beside me."

Brandon patted the couch and Peanut hopped up and snuggled down by Grandma.

"I think he likes me. Maybe I remind him of the old lady he used to live with." Grandma was pleased.

"He still stinks," Brandon said. "But not as bad as he used to. We want to bathe him in your big shower. Maybe if we keep bathing him he will soon smell better."

It was a busy day at Grandma's house. Toward evening Mama showered Grandma. Then Jeneva bathed Peanut. He shook wildly and water flew all over the shower. Next he ran out to the living room and rolled on a towel, rubbing himself against it to get dry. Grandma and the children laughed and laughed at his antics. Then Jeneva took him outside and let him run around in the fresh air to finish drying.

It was nearly dark by the time supper was over, the dishes washed, and the floors swept. Jeneva went outside to get Peanut. A few minutes later she opened the kitchen door, out of breath and worried. "I called and called but Peanut doesn't come. I looked at the shop and in the barn, but he's nowhere."

Everyone but Grandma hurried outside to help look. Peanut wasn't at the neighbors. He wasn't penned in the shop. He wasn't hiding under the porch.

Finally Mama told the children to get into the van. "Grandma can call us if she hears Peanut scratching on her door. Let's drive up and down the road and look on all the neighbors' porches. He's not used to being here. Maybe he can't remember how to get back to Grandma's house."

A sad group of children climbed into the van. No happy

"Maybe if we keep bathing him he will soon smell better."

dog sat on the floor.

"I'm sorry about Peanut," Grandma told Mama. "Tell the children I can't help look, but I can pray."

Mama drove slowly around the little village. There was no fluffy brown dog anywhere. By now it was very dark. Mama parked the van in the little driveway that went to Grandpa's oil well. "Let's pray and then look at Grandma's again," she said. "Maybe Peanut is back there.

"Dear God," Mama prayed, "you see our little dog right now and know where he is—even if we don't. Keep him safe and help us find him if it's your will. Amen."

I wish Mama wouldn't say 'if it's your will' when she prays. I just want to find Peanut, Jeneva thought. *But I need to accept God's will—even if I don't feel like it.*

By now Brandon was crying. He was sure he would never see his little pet again. "I want Daddy," he wailed.

Mama drove into Grandma's lane to look one more time. But there was no little dog on the porch. There was nothing to do but go home.

Daddy stood at the door to welcome his family. He was sorry to hear his children's sad tale. "I'll drive around and tell a few neighbors to watch for Peanut and call us if they see him. He's so new, the neighbors don't know he belongs to us."

Daddy drove away and a group of sorrowful children got ready for bed.

"Will Peanut get scared and cold tonight?" Jolynn wondered.

"Maybe he will make a warm nest with leaves," Jeneva said hopefully.

When Mama came to the girls' room to say "good night," she reminded them to pray.

Several days went by. Every day the children prayed Peanut would be found.

"I think he's a goner," Mama finally told them.

Then one day the phone rang. Jolynn answered and listened a little. She gave a joyful shout and dropped the receiver into its holder. "Grandma said Peanut is at her house. Let's go get him!" She jumped up and down in anticipation.

"Calm down," Mama said. "What is going on? Are you sure that's what Grandma said?"

"Yes, she said, 'Come get Peanut.' I know she did."

"I'll call her," Mama said. "I can't believe it!"

"We've been praying," Brandon reminded her.

And it was true. Grandma told Mama that Peanut was running around in her living room.

It didn't take any coaxing to get the Yoder children out the door this time. They were on the road in minutes. "Drive faster, Mama," Brandon begged.

"No sense driving so fast we end up in the ditch," Mama said.

It was a wild scramble as everyone raced to unbuckle and be first into Grandma's house. And there was Peanut!

"How did he get here?"

"Do you think he missed us?"

"Where was he all this time?"

Peanut loved the attention. He barked and ran in circles. He whined with happiness and wiggled loose from the arms that tried to squeeze him.

"A lady knocked on my door," Grandma explained. "I was so surprised when she came in with Peanut in her arms. She saw a dog beside the road and stopped. He jumped into her car and rode home with her. When she saw how clean and well behaved he was, she knew he was someone's pet. So she came back to this neighborhood to find his owner. This was the first house she stopped at. I told her I will have some happy grandchildren."

Well, that's like a story from a book, Jeneva thought. *Except it's really true and it happened to us.*

"I wonder if that lady actually stole him and all our prayers made her feel guilty until she brought Peanut back," Jolynn speculated.

"Jolynn! Let's just say, 'Thank you, God' and not accuse anyone of stealing," Mama said.

"Yes, God answered our prayers," Jeneva rejoiced. "Mama said, 'He's a goner,' but he isn't."

"All this time we thought he was cold and hungry or dead and he was just living with someone else," Jolynn marveled.

"I'm glad your dog is back," Grandma told the children. "Don't forget to thank God for answering your prayers."

"Yeah, and it was even according to my will," Jeneva rejoiced.

CHAPTER 10

A Snowman for Grandma

"Supper time," Mama called.

Everyone hurried to the table. "Chili soup!" Jolynn cheered.

"And corn bread!" Jeneva added.

"Let's pray," Daddy said and everyone quieted. "Heavenly Father, thank you for being with us through this day and bringing us safely back together again this evening. Thank you for our warm house and this food that Mama cooked. Bless all those who are less fortunate than we are. In Jesus' name, Amen."

Daddy had hardly said, "Amen," when Jeneva blurted, "Listen to the wind."

"Is that what you were thinking about during prayer?" he asked.

"Maybe," Jeneva admitted sheepishly.

"It's cold." Jolynn shivered. "I feel wind coming in around the patio door." She jumped up and pulled the electric heater closer to her chair.

Another blast of wind shook the door. "Snow! I see snowflakes," Jeneva whooped. "Think we'll get three inches?"

"I predict a foot," Brandon said hopefully.

At bedtime the children peered out the windows. The ground was covered except for patches where the wind swept it bare. The wind died down during the night, but snow continued to fall. The sun came up to smile on a beautiful, glistening world.

Brandon was the first to wake. "Why aren't the girls up yet?" he asked Mama.

"There's no school today so I let them sleep," Mama said. "But you may wake them. It's time for them to get up."

Brandon hurried to the girls' room. "Girls, get up. There's a surprise! No school today. It's too snowy."

The girls bounded out of their beds. Snow! They had forgotten about snow while they slept. They rushed to the patio door. "Oh!" Jolynn squealed. "There's lots of snow."

"Let's go out and play," Brandon suggested.

"What about breakfast?" But no one heard Mama's question. Not with all that snow waiting to be played in.

The children rushed this way and that collecting coats and boots. "Wait for me. Wait for me!" Betty called as she tried to zip her coat with gloved hands.

Jeneva turned back and yanked up the zipper. Betty tramped out and slammed the door.

Mama put a kettle of milk on the stove to heat. Cold little people would enjoy hot chocolate with their breakfast.

Later Mama heard a knock. She looked out the door and saw a cute little snowman poised on the deck rail. "For you!" the children chorused.

"Thank you. He is so cute! Are you ready for breakfast now?" Soon the hungry troop was gathered at the table, drinking hot chocolate.

"It's fun to play in the snow," said Jeneva.

"I'm going to call Grandma to tell her about no school today," Jolynn planned aloud.

"Poor Grandma can't play in the snow," Brandon said soberly.

"I have an idea," Mama said. "You children could make another little snowman for Grandma."

"Yes, yes!" the children chorused.

"Could we make snow cream for her too?" Jolynn asked.

"Sure," Mama agreed. "Let's do our morning work first. Then we can take Grandma some snow to enjoy."

The children planned as they worked. Soon they were back outside, building another little snowman. They scooped clean snow into a dishpan for snow cream. Mama brought a pie plate outside for the snowman to sit in. She also had a container of frozen raspberries.

"Oh, good!" the children cheered. "Raspberry snow cream."

"Hop into the truck," Mama said. "The roads are slippery. We better have four-wheel-drive so we don't end up in the ditch." It was three miles to Grandma's house. Mama drove slowly.

"I'm cold," Betty whimpered.

"The heater doesn't work in this old truck," Mama told her.

"Good thing it doesn't or our snow would melt," Jeneva said.

The children tramped into Grandma's toasty warm house. "Surprise for you, Grandma!" they called. Jeneva placed the pie plate with the snowman on Grandma's lap.

Mama poured a little milk into the dishpan full of snow. Next she added several clumps of brown sugar, a big splash of vanilla, and the raspberries. Jolynn got out bowls and spoons and everyone enjoyed the treat.

"Thank you for bringing some snow to me since I

can't go out and enjoy it," Grandma told the children. "Wheelchairs and snow don't mix very well."

"That's right," Mama agreed. "I don't like to take Grandma out when it's snowy. I'm afraid I will slip and the wheelchair will get away from me and Grandma will get dumped into the snow."

Grandma laughed. "Then I would look like a snowman."

The children laughed too. Then they put their winter wraps back on and headed home for more fun in the snow.

"Thank you for bringing some snow to me . . ."

CHAPTER 11

Patience and Play Dough

Winter slowly slipped away into spring. A leisurely Saturday morning breakfast was finished. "How about working in the barn loft as soon as we wash these dishes?" Jeneva asked Jolynn.

"Suits me fine," her sister answered. They had started cleaning the junk out of the barn loft in hopes of making a place to play on rainy days. This would be a perfect day to work at that project.

Mama walked into the kitchen. "Girls," she said, "it doesn't suit anyone else to stay with Grandma today. I think you are old enough to stay with her several hours. I will take you over and help you get settled, and later this afternoon I will come back to shower Grandma and help you finish up the day."

Jeneva's brow puckered. "I don't want to go to Grandma's house," she said crossly. "It's Saturday, the only day we can work at the barn. It's so boring at Grandma's, and when Grandpa isn't in the shop I get scared."

"What if the house starts on fire? How would we get Grandma out?" Jolynn's feelings matched her older sister's.

Mama studied the two stormy faces. "I didn't know this was about having fun," she said soberly. "It's about taking care of Grandma. A life of service isn't about us and what we want to do. It's about doing what we know we should do for others."

Mama's eyes softened with understanding. "There are days I don't feel like going to Grandma's house either. Sometimes I have so much work to do at home I wonder how I can be gone a whole day. But Grandma didn't choose to be handicapped. We need to care for her as cheerfully as possible. God will help us do the work He has given us, girls."

Jeneva looked more closely at Mama. She seemed tired. *I never knew that sometimes Mama wishes she didn't need to go to Grandma's. If she can do it, I can do it too.* Then she had an idea.

"I saw a new recipe for play dough," Jeneva said. "May

I take it along and make it at Grandma's?"

"Yes, that's a good idea," Mama said.

Jolynn saw Jeneva was trying to be cheerful. "Will Grandpa be in the shop?"

"Yes, I called him. He will be there all day. I know you don't like to be there without an adult. I can understand how that feels," Mama said. "When I was young I used to be scared when it got dark and Grandpa wasn't home. One time a drunk driver crashed into the fence by our house and ran away from the police. I was scared he would come back and burst our house door open."

If Mama stayed with Grandma when she was young, then maybe I can be brave enough if Grandpa is close by, Jolynn thought. "Could we invite a friend? That would make it more fun."

"How about Emily? I can call her mom and see if it would suit," Mama said.

The girls brightened. Emily's mom said she could bike over in about an hour.

At Grandma's house, Mama cleaned up the kitchen. Jolynn made Grandma her morning cup of coffee with a little sugar and plenty of cream. Jeneva got out a kettle and started her play dough.

"When will Emily get here?" Jolynn asked.

"Before long, I suppose," Mama said.

Mama sat at the kitchen table and rested her head in

her hands. "Is something wrong?" Grandma asked.

"I got up this morning with a headache and so far coffee and Tylenol haven't helped," Mama answered. She looked at the kettle of goop Jeneva was stirring on the stove. "Jeneva Grace! What's wrong with your play dough?"

"It was so thick I decided to add another cup of water," Jeneva said. She stirred vigorously, trying not to get splashed by the bubbling, hot liquid.

"You put in two cups of water?" Mama got up from the table for a better look at the recipe and the mixture sloshing in the kettle. "You can't expect something to turn out if you don't follow the recipe."

Mama dumped more flour into the kettle and took the spoon from Jeneva. She turned the heat lower and stirred as fast as she could. "I wish you would learn to work in one spot instead of on the table, on the counter, and beside the stove. Everywhere you went you made a mess."

Jeneva looked down, and her shoulders drooped. She swallowed the lump in her throat. When Mama noticed her stricken look, she stopped stirring so fast. Her voice softened. "I'm sorry, Jeneva. I shouldn't be so cross. Messes can be wiped up."

Jeneva looked up bravely. "It's alright, Mama. I should have followed the recipe."

"Well, let's look on the bright side," Mama said. "With twice as much play dough, you have plenty to share."

Just then Emily bounced in the door. Her red hair curled around her forehead and her flushed cheeks made her freckles show. "Good morning, Grandma Myrtle," she greeted.

"You look like you had a fast bike ride," Grandma said.

"Yes. I had to clean up my room before I came, and it took me a long time so I rode as fast as I could to get here." Emily sat down on the recliner and took deep breaths.

After Mama left, the girls ran errands and played games. Jolynn mixed Kool-Aid and poured it into tall glasses. Grandma drank hers from her sipper cup. The girls had fun creating a zoo of strange-looking play dough animals and cutting shapes with cookie cutters.

At lunchtime, they chose from the wide variety of leftovers and heated them on the stove. When Grandpa saw the full table he said, "You girls made enough for an army. How much did you think I could eat?"

"We are hungry too," Emily said. She watched as Grandpa filled his plate. "Now I know why you are plump," she teased.

Grandpa's loud, jolly laugh filled the kitchen. "Watch what you say or I'll put your head between your ears."

"It already is!" Emily retorted playfully.

Mama came back at four o'clock. "How was your day?"

"It was good," Jolynn said. "We had fun."

The girls had fun . . . cutting shapes with cookie cutters.

"Did they take good care of you?" Mama asked Grandma.

"Yes, they did. My granddaughters are growing up." Grandma said.

"At lunch time Jolynn cooked Grandpa's beans so long they looked funny. But he ate them anyway," Jeneva said.

Mama laughed. "It probably brought back memories of when his girls were learning to cook. We burned food and boiled things over in the oven and made cakes that didn't rise. But he didn't complain. He ate our food anyhow and doesn't seem any worse for it."

"Let's help each other get this place cleaned up," Mama said.

Emily and Jolynn emptied the dishwasher. Jeneva tidied up the living room. Mama scrubbed the five kettles that were soaking in the sink. The girls swept the floors while Mama prepared supper.

Soon the house was in order. Grandma Myrtle was showered and settled on the couch with her embroidery and her sipper cup of water. The phone was close by in case she needed something before Grandpa came in.

"Thank you, girls," Grandma called as they were going out the door. "And thank you, Emily, for coming for the day. Having you here made the day more interesting. Be safe riding home."

"You're welcome," the girls called back.

CHAPTER 12

Spray Bottles and Shopping

"Betty, can you bring Grandma's wheelchair, please?" Mama asked. Betty was four years old now, and big enough to help.

Betty hurried to Grandma's bedroom where the wheelchair was kept. She pushed it to the couch and locked the brakes. Mama moved Grandma from the couch and settled her in the chair.

Mama took Grandma's hairpins out and started to brush the snarls.

"Can I help?" Betty begged.

"Maybe you could get the water bottle and spray the front of Grandma's hair," Mama said.

Betty went to the cupboard in Grandma's bedroom. Soon she was back with the water bottle. She began vigorously wetting the front of Grandma's hair. Little streams of water ran down Grandma's face.

"Betty, stop! Stop!" Mama exclaimed when she saw how it was raining on Grandma. "Look at Grandma's glasses." Mama took the dripping glasses off Grandma's face and dried them with a paper towel.

Betty ran to the bathroom for a clean wash cloth. She carefully wiped Grandma's face. "I'm sorry," she said cheerfully.

Grandma laughed. "It's alright. You had fun spraying, and now my face is washed for the day." When the glasses were back on her face, she said, "My! This sure looks better. My glasses needed a good cleaning."

Betty hopped up on the footrests of the wheelchair and bounced. "Grandma, I'm going with you to the dentist," she said.

Grandma's chair bucked on an extra-hard bounce. "Betty!" Mama protested.

"And then Mama said we are taking you to Walmart to shop. Won't that be fun?" Betty chattered on. Then she lost her balance and plopped backward onto the floor. She sat there and watched while Mama put pins in Grandma's covering.

"Are you Mama's helper today?" Grandma asked.

"Yes, she is." Mama answered. "And she's a good helper if she's not too bouncy."

Betty opened the front door and Mama guided Grandma's chair down the ramp toward the big white van. Betty ran ahead and opened the side door and pushed the button that made the handicap lift go up and down. Nothing happened. "It doesn't work," she said.

"Yes, it does, but you have to turn the switch on." Mama said.

Betty turned the silver switch and put the lift down. Then she hopped on for a ride up. Mama strapped Grandma's wheelchair in place so it couldn't roll while the van was driving. Soon Mama was parking in a handicap parking space at the dentist's office.

Betty sat beside Mama in the waiting room. After what seemed like a long wait, a nurse opened a door and called, "Myrtle Petre."

"That's us," Betty said. She followed Mama and Grandma back a long, wide hall. The nurse backed Grandma's chair into a little room and put on a pair of blue rubber gloves.

"What can I do for you today?" the nurse asked.

"My teeth are rubbing my gums," Grandma explained.

"Let me have a look." The nurse took Grandma's false teeth out and shone a light into Grandma's mouth. "Oh, yes, I can see a sore spot in the back." She reached into

Grandma's mouth. "Right here?"

Grandma jumped. "Yes, right there."

"I'll file this rough spot off your dentures and see if that helps any." The nurse carried Grandma's teeth to the counter where all sorts of interesting tools were kept. She picked up a small grinder that looked just like the big steel grinder Grandpa had in his mechanic shop. Carefully she shaved off little pieces. Betty watched in fascination while the nurse rinsed the teeth and put them back in Grandma's mouth.

"That feels better. Thank you!" Grandma Myrtle said.

The nurse led the way out with Mama pushing Grandma's chair and Betty following them. The nurse stopped at the receptionist's desk and reached for a pretty glass bowl of candy. Betty chose a white piece, and Grandma reached for a piece with red and white stripes.

"I want to match with Grandma," Betty said.

The nurse dug to the bottom of the bowl and found a red and white piece. She handed it to Betty. "Just keep both pieces," she said. "You look like you are being a good helper today."

Betty opened the door and Mama pushed Grandma to the van. "Do you like to go to Walmart, Grandma?" Betty asked as she and Grandma rode the lift.

"Yes, I do. But I rarely go shopping. Today I want to look for some birthday gifts."

"I'll push the cart," Betty promised, though she had to walk on tiptoes to see over the cart handle.

It took a long time for Grandma and Mama to decide what to buy. The cart got fuller and fuller. Betty pushed it from one aisle to the next. "Mama, this cart is too heavy. I'm getting tired. May I push Grandma?"

"You can try. But be careful, you won't be able to see over Grandma's shoulders. You might crash into something and hurt Grandma," Mama cautioned.

Betty grasped the wheelchair handles and began pushing Grandma. Mama pushed the heavy shopping cart. "Betty, turn quickly!" Mama grabbed the arm of the chair just in time. The wheelchair swerved and missed a big post. "Be careful."

"Grandma, you better watch and tell me not to hit things," Betty said.

At the front of the store, Mama checked her list. "Oh, I forgot shampoo. Park Grandma here and come with me, Betty. The shampoo is at the back of the store."

"Mama, I better stay with Grandma," Betty said. "If we leave her alone, someone might kidnap her."

Mama laughed. "Oh, I doubt that. But you may stay here beside her if you want to guard her."

Betty parked Grandma's chair beside the cart while Mama hurried to find shampoo. After they paid for their cartload of things, Betty pushed Grandma through the

"If we leave her alone, someone might kidnap her."

automatic doors and across the parking lot. Betty climbed into her booster with a contented sigh. "I'm really tired," she said as she strapped herself in. "But it was fun to shop with you, Grandma."

"I enjoyed shopping too," Grandma said. "I wasn't even very scared when you pushed my chair."

The shoppers were scarcely out of town when Mama looked in the rearview mirror. "I guess Betty *is* tired. She's already asleep."

"I feel a little tired too," Grandma said. "I'll be glad to get home to my couch for a nap. Thank you for taking me to town today."

CHAPTER 13

Minnows and Whales

Daddy bent over the water fountain in the shop and took a long, cold drink. The door behind him opened, letting in the warm sunshine, and four children rushed in.

"Daddy, can we go fishing?"

"Please, Daddy? Mama will help us dig the worms."

Daddy straightened and wiped his mouth on his shirt sleeve.

"May we? May we?"

"What if I say no?" Daddy asked.

"Daddy!" Brandon wailed.

"He's teasing. I know he is," Jolynn squealed. "His eyes

are twinkling."

Daddy laughed. "Yes, we can go fishing. One of you could invite Grandpas to go with us. We should leave at 5:30 so we can fish awhile before dark."

Jolynn didn't hear Daddy's last sentence. She was already running toward the house.

"Come, Brandon, let's get the shovel and a container for worms," Jeneva planned as she headed for the garage.

Soon Mama came out, and Betty ran ahead of her to the garden. "I want to hold a worm," she called.

"Let's dig in the potato patch first," Mama said. "The mulch is thick and there are probably worms hiding in the loose dirt." Mama dug up shovels full of dirt while the children pulled out long worms. They seemed to shrink when they were dropped into the plastic container, and they wiggled around trying to find a place to hide.

"Oh, I want that big one!" Betty exclaimed. "I know I could catch a fish with it." She cupped her hands to cradle her trophy.

Takes more than big worms to catch a fish, Jeneva thought. *Betty hops around so much a fish would have to be stupid to get caught on her hook . . . But that's not kind. I really do hope she catches a fish.*

"I think we have enough," Brandon said after a few more shovels full of dirt had been inspected for worms.

"We better get a few more," Jolynn said. "Daddy says

we feed the fish more than we catch them."

Daddy loaded the tackle box and fishing poles onto the back of the truck. Brandon brought the camp chairs from the basement. The girls scurried around, helping to finish the picnic supper and loading the big basket with plates and cups.

I better not make the tea too sweet, Jolynn thought as she watched the tiny grains of sugar swirl and dissolve. *Grandpa will call it hummingbird water.*

Daddy added the little grill to the growing pile on the truck and everyone climbed in. Peanut scrambled into the cab with them and Brandon slammed the door.

"Grandpa said he will meet us at the pond," Jolynn said.

"Did you tell him what time?" Daddy asked.

"No, I didn't know any time," Jolynn said dolefully.

"You ran so fast to go call that you never heard Daddy say a time," Jeneva said.

"He called back and asked," Mama comforted Jolynn.

It took only a few minutes to drive to the pond. "Grandpa beat us!" Betty exclaimed. Grandpa's big white van was parked on the bank. A pair of barn swallows flitted about over the water.

"Oh, look! Grandpa bought worms from the little store," Jeneva rejoiced. "I like boughten worms better than homemade ones because they are fatter."

Grandpa was unloading Grandma. His red camp chair

and fishing pole were already settled by the shore.

"Grandpa, we have worms too!" Betty yelled as she jumped from the truck.

Grandpa laughed. "Well, the fish are probably all scared to the other side of the pond the way you yelled. You'll have to be quiet if you want to catch fish."

Betty looked crestfallen. "I brought my own worm," she whispered. She opened her clammy hand and showed Grandpa her long, fat worm. It barely wiggled.

Grandpa forgot about being quiet. He threw back his head and laughed. The trees across the pond echoed back at him. "That worm had a rough ride getting here, but maybe it will catch a fish."

There was a lot of racket until everyone had a chair, a pole, and a worm. Then they settled down and tried to be quiet. "I saw a fish," Jolynn whispered excitedly.

Peanut did not understand about being quiet. He rushed to the edge of the pond and barked. "Peanut, hush," Jeneva scolded. Peanut backed up and sat down, then let out another bark.

Jeneva sighed. She put down her pole, snapped the leash onto Peanut's collar, and tried to pull him up the bank. He planted his feet and locked his brakes. "Peanut, bad dog," she scolded. Slowly, stubbornly, he crept up the bank. Jeneva hooked his leash on Grandma's wheelchair handle. "Sit," she said sternly. Peanut sat. His tail hung down and his ears lay flat against his head.

"He isn't too happy about being hooked to me," Grandma laughed. "You are a good dog," she comforted. Peanut's ears perked and he flopped at Grandma's feet with a little sigh.

"Don't pity him too much, Grandma. It's his own fault," Jolynn said tartly.

Suddenly Betty squealed. "Grandpa caught a fish!"

Grandpa pulled it in. "An overgrown minnow," he guffawed. He unhooked the small fish and tossed it back in.

"Brandon, your line is jerking," Daddy said. Brandon reeled in as fast as he could. "Nothing," he said in disappointment. "Even my worm is gone."

"That's why we dug plenty," Jeneva reminded him.

Jolynn reeled her line in. "Mine is gone too," she said. Carefully she fastened another worm onto her hook. All was quiet for a few minutes until a shout from Betty got everyone's attention. "I have a fish!" she yelled. She leaped wildly and ran backward up the bank, dragging her fish to the shore.

"Slow down, slow down!" Daddy called. He took Betty's pole and reeled in the line. A little bluegill dangled from the hook.

"I want to hold it. Give it to me," Betty said. She tried to hold the slippery fish but lost her grasp and it fell into the grass.

Peanut barked and barked. Grandma's wheelchair gave little jerks as he pulled against his leash. "It's a good thing my brakes are locked or I think Peanut would take off with me," Grandma said. "He wants that fish for his supper."

"I'd be ready for some supper." Daddy laid his fishing pole on the back of the truck and unloaded the grill. Soon he had hamburgers and hotdogs sizzling. Mama got out the picnic basket.

"We need a table for our food," Jeneva said.

Grandma looked around. "I have an idea. Unfold my lift and set the food on it."

Daddy took Grandma up on her offer, arranging the grilled meat, bread, and other foods on the lift. "Supper!" Daddy's voice rang out across the water.

When Brandon saw the hotdogs, he said, "I don't want that one. It's burnt."

"I'll eat it," Grandpa said. "A little bit of carbon never hurt anyone." He put the blackened hotdog on a bun and added a thick squirt of ketchup.

Jolynn tried to stab a fat pickle from the jar. It wobbled and tipped over. Juice ran through the lift grate and soaked into the grass. *This is a good table*, she thought. *We don't have to wipe up the spills.*

After supper Mama cleaned away the food and sat down beside Grandma.

"Everyone but me caught a fish," Jeneva complained.

"Try fishing over by Grandpa," Daddy suggested.

Jeneva baited her hook and cast out her line. Soon a fish nibbled. She set the hook and reeled in as fast as she could, but her hook was empty. *This is nothing but a waste of worms.* Slowly she baited her hook again. She dangled it in the air and bounced it from side to side. The worm spun in circles. She forgot all about Grandpa.

Suddenly Grandpa jerked and yelped, "Watch your hook!" Jeneva's hook had snagged Grandpa's shirt sleeve. He pushed the hook out of the material and rubbed the small scratch on his arm. "Are you trying to catch fish or a whale?"

Jeneva laughed so hard she sat down in the grass. "Well, you are more of a whale than an overgrown minnow," she teased.

Grandpa's jolly laugh echoed from the trees. "I think it's time to get Grandma home out of this chilly evening air and before you do worse damage," he said.

"It's fun to fish with Grandpa," Brandon said as they rode home. "I like how he calls the little fish overgrown minnows."

"I think Grandpas enjoyed the evening, and it does Grandma good to get outside," Mama said. "Maybe we can invite them again sometime."

CHAPTER 14

Shower Time

"Shower time for Grandma." Mama called. "Who will bring her shower chair?"

"Me!" Jolynn called from the playroom upstairs.

"Me!" Betty echoed, hurrying down the stairs. "I beat!"

Mama jumped aside as the chair sped toward her ankles. "Slow down!" she cautioned. "But thanks for bringing the chair."

Grandma laughed. "My chairs can be dangerous. I don't know how many times my caregiver's toes have been run over." Sometimes the chair went over Grandma's toes too, but it did not hurt her very much. The nerves in Grandma's body didn't send clear messages to her brain.

Grandma was lying on the couch. If she lay or sat in one position too long, her body became stiff.

Mama carefully bent Grandma's legs at the knees until her feet rested on the floor. She grasped Grandma under the arms and slowly pulled her into a sitting position. "Does that hurt, Grandma?" Brandon wondered.

"No, it doesn't," Grandma said. "My muscles are stiff, but if they are stretched out slowly it doesn't hurt."

After Grandma was sitting comfortably on the couch, Mama locked the wheels on the shower chair.

"Why did you lock the brakes?" Brandon asked.

"To keep the chair from rolling away when I sit Grandma on it," Mama said. "One time I pushed the chair up to the couch and was going to sit Grandma on it. Before I locked the brakes, I had to go do something else. When Aunt Edith tried to put Grandma on the chair, it rolled away. Grandma crashed to the floor and Edith landed on top of her."

"Grandma! Did you get hurt?" Brandon asked.

"Not much," Grandma said. "I had a headache and my nose hurt where it was hit by my glasses. But I don't want to try that again today, especially since I just had kidney stone surgery."

"I don't feel like falling on top of you either." Mama maneuvered Grandma safely from the couch to the chair. She untangled Grandma's foot from the long tube attached to a jug and set the jug on Grandma's lap. A few stitches kept the tube from slipping from the hole in Grandma's back. "This drain tube for your kidneys is annoying," Mama said.

"You aren't the only one tired of this apparatus," Grandma consoled. "Hopefully next week the doctor can take the tube out."

"I'll pull Grandma's chair," Jolynn offered. Together, she and Mama maneuvered Grandma from the living room into the master bedroom and bathroom. Jolynn parked Grandma in the shower and went to the dresser to get a gown and warm socks.

"I can help wash Grandma," Betty said. She got a towel and two washcloths out of the cupboard.

"I have plenty of nurses even when I'm not in the hospital," Grandma said.

Mama turned the water on so it could get warm. She tied her skirt in a knot so it would not drag on the wet shower floor.

"Tie mine up too," Betty begged. Mama turned to tie Betty's skirt and gasped.

"That is too much soap!" she said when she saw the puddle of soap Betty had squirted on her washcloth. "Here. Put some on my wash cloth."

"Well, I want Grandma to smell good," Betty said.

"You can wash Grandma's feet and legs," Mama said.

"I will wash the rest of her."

Mama carefully taped plastic wrap over the big bandage on Grandma's back. Her incisions needed to stay clean and dry to keep from getting infected.

Betty reached for the shower wand and began spraying Grandma's shoulders. "Careful," Grandma cautioned. "I get dizzy if too much water gets inside my ears."

Mama took the wand and hung it up.

"Does your back hurt, Grandma?" Jolynn asked tenderly.

"Not too much, unless it gets bumped. That's why your mama tries to move me around so carefully."

After Grandma was scrubbed clean and wiped dry, Mama took the bandage off. In the middle of a large purple bruise were two little cuts held together by black stitches.

"Oh!" Betty exclaimed. "It's ugly. Why is it all purple?"

"While Grandma was sleeping, the doctor made these two little cuts," Mama explained. "The doctor inserted his instruments, and then removed the kidney stones after they were crushed. That made a bruise, but it will get better in a week or two."

"You poor Grandma." Betty patted Grandma's leg.

Mama wiped around the incisions with an alcohol pad. She put salve and a clean bandage over the bruised area and covered everything with soft tape.

While Jolynn rubbed lotion on Grandma's feet, she

noticed the scars on them and remembered why they were there. When Uncle Ezra had suffered so much from leukemia, it had been a stressful time for the whole family. God had chozen to heal Uncle Ez in heaven instead of on earth. Now Aunt Edith was alone with her two little girls.

"Remember how sick you were after Ez died?" Jolynn looked up at Grandma.

Grandma nodded slowly. "Yes, I felt so helpless while Ez was dying," she reminisced. "It was hard to see my daughter suffer while the cancer took her husband."

Grandma had become very sick after Ez's funeral. The stress and grief were too much for her weak body and she got a skin disease called bullosis. Her legs and feet swelled and the skin peeled off. For several weeks Mama and her sisters bandaged Grandma until new skin grew back. Now there were only scars.

Hmm. I never thought of that before. I only thought of how Edith and her girls felt when Ez died— and how much I miss him, Jolynn reflected as she pulled warm socks onto Grandma's feet. *But Grandma suffered in a different way. I'm glad she is feeling better now.*

"I'll put your spray on you," Betty offered. She reached for the body spray and sprayed vigorously.

"Stop, stop!" Mama sputtered. "You got it in my face. It smells good, but it tastes awful."

"Mama, help me." Betty's voice brought Jolynn's mind

back to Grandma's bedroom. Betty had pulled Grandma's gown over her head and was puffing as she struggled to put Grandma's arm into the sleeve. It fell limply to the side. She struggled harder. Nothing worked.

Mama reached her hand into the bottom of the sleeve and grasped Grandma's wrist. She pulled the sleeve smoothly up Grandma's arm. "You have to know how," Grandma teased Betty.

Betty reached into the drawer for a comb. She combed back Grandma's hair, trying to do it gently. She pinned on Grandma's head covering and then Grandma was ready to be wheeled to the living room.

Soon Grandma was sitting on the couch again. Her feet were propped on a little chair and a fuzzy blanket covered her legs.

"You look nice and fresh, Grandma," Brandon said.

"Thank you," Grandma replied. "I feel fresh and clean."

"And she smells good, thanks to Betty," Mama said as she turned to the kitchen to finish supper.

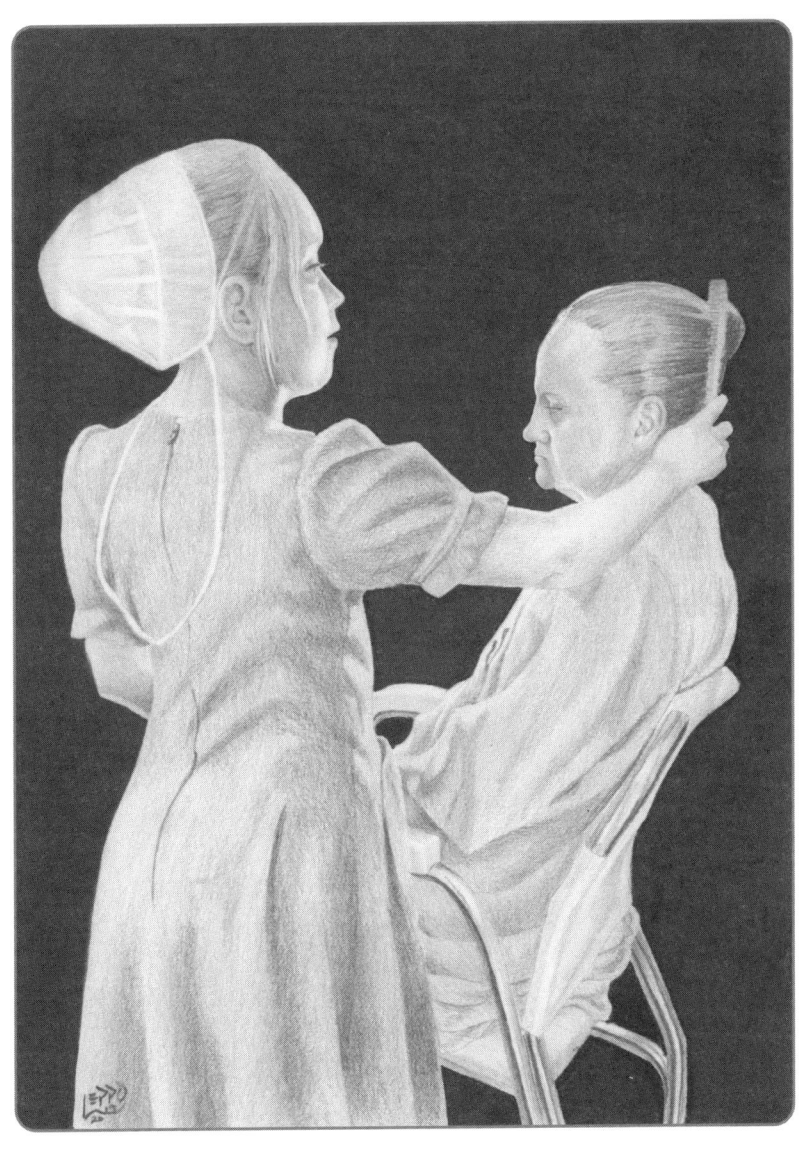

Betty combed back Grandma's hair, trying to do it gently.

CHAPTER 15

Choosing Willingness

"Who is going with me to take Grandma for lab work?" Mama called.

"I am," Jolynn answered.

"Me too," Betty said as the girls came hurrying from their bedroom.

"I'll stay here with Dad," Brandon decided. He dashed out the door, hopped on his bike, and sped toward the shop.

Jeneva was at the clothesline hanging up the last of the wet towels. It was getting warmer as the sun climbed higher. She dreamed of relaxing in the cool living room with a book. Mama's voice broke into her thoughts. "I'm taking Grandma for labs," Mama called. "Do you want to go along?"

"I'll soon be done. If you wait, I'll go along," Jeneva answered. Quickly she pinned the last few items to the line and dashed for the house while the others loaded into the van.

"Where did Jeneva go?" Mama asked as she backed out of the garage. Then the house door opened and Jeneva strolled to the van, her nose already buried in a book.

"Slowpoke," Jolynn greeted as Jeneva slid into her seat.

"Slowpoke," Betty echoed.

"Mama, make them stop!" Jeneva complained.

"Girls, be quiet. All of you," Mama said.

Grandma's niece had come to care for her for several weeks, so Grandma was already dressed and ready to go when they arrived. Mama lifted Grandma into her wheelchair and pushed her out to the big white van.

"I'm sitting up front," Jeneva said as she dashed for the front seat.

"So what," Jolynn retorted. "I was planning to run the lift, anyhow." She opened the side door and flipped the switches to lower the lift. Mama pushed Grandma onto the lift and Jolynn gave her a ride up. Carefully they fastened the straps and then they were off to town.

"I hope the fat nurse gives me Band-aids," Betty said.

"Don't ever say she's fat when she can hear you," Jolynn cautioned.

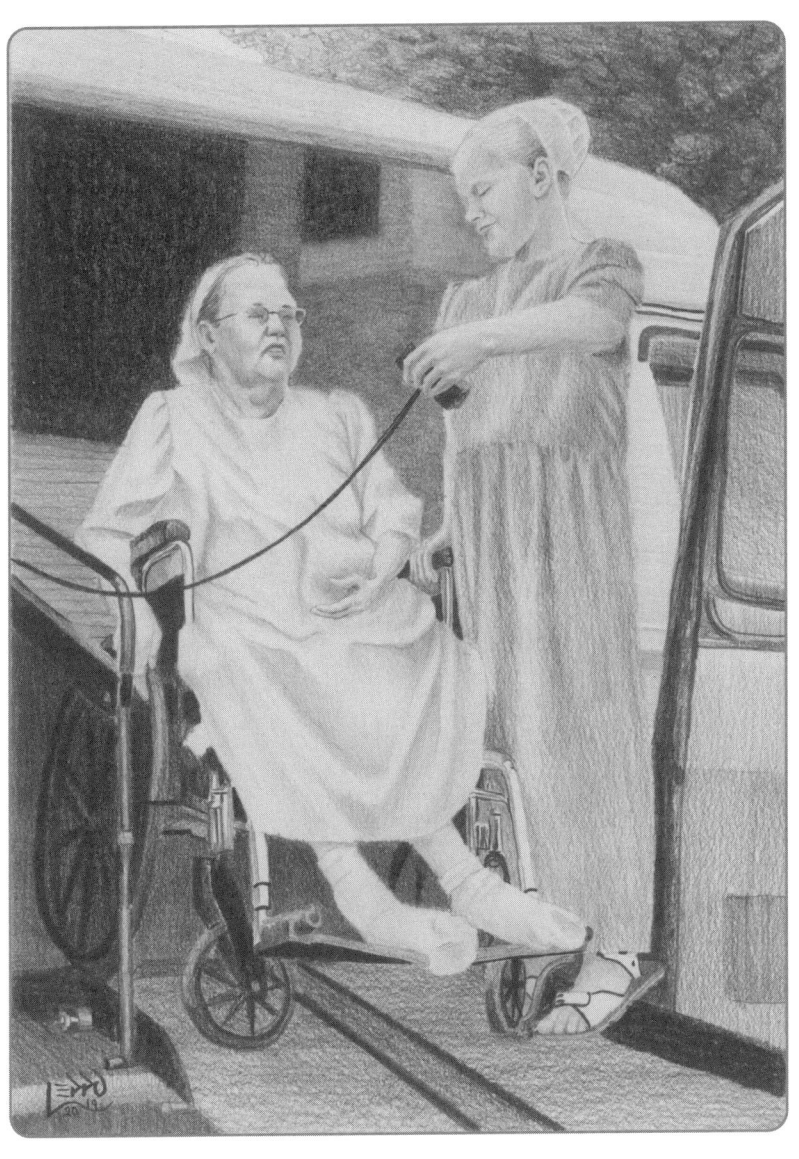

"I was planning to run the lift, anyhow."

"I won't!" Betty promised. "She's nice even if she is fat."

"She's a blessing," Grandma told the girls. "She's one of the few nurses who can find my blood veins."

An hour later Grandma was back on her couch. Betty had the Band-aids she had been hoping for, plus a few stickers for herself and Brandon. Jeneva and Jolynn were in a more companionable mood.

"See you tonight," Mama said as she tucked a blanket around Grandma.

"Why did you say you would see her tonight?" Jolynn asked as they drove home.

"The Miller family is having a yard sale this weekend and the church ladies are invited to come tonight and have first chance to buy things."

"That sounds fun. May we go along?" Jeneva asked.

"Sure," Mama promised.

"Are you taking Grandma?" Jolynn asked.

"Yes," Mama replied.

Jolynn scowled. "I get so tired of taking Grandma places. Why can't Aunt Edith do it this time?"

"Jolynn," Mama scolded. "That will be enough from you. Aunt Edith helps a lot with Grandma. But since Uncle Ezra died, it's not as easy for her. She is a widow with two little girls to care for and I have two big girls to help me with Grandma."

Jolynn chewed on her lip the way she always did when

she was upset, but she was quiet.

"When you children were small, it was harder for me to take Grandma places," Mama went on. "I didn't have anyone to open doors and help with the lift. But Aunt Edith didn't have any children then, and she used to take Grandma places so I didn't have to."

"I know," Jolynn relented. "Most of the time I don't mind, but sometimes I get tired of it."

"Do you know I feel like that, too?" Mama asked. "Sometimes I look at my friends and wonder how it must be to have a mother who could come and help me instead of me going to help her."

Jolynn looked up in surprise, but she thought about Mama's words. "It's okay, Mama. We can all help each other."

"Yes, dear, we can." Mama reached over to pat Jolynn's shoulder.

CHAPTER 16

A New Body—Someday

"I heard the mailman stop," Grandma called. "Do I have a granddaughter who will get the mail for me?"

"I'll go," Jeneva offered. Slowly she walked down the lane, carrying her open book. She looked both ways before crossing the road. She stopped reading long enough to look into Grandma's mailbox. She pulled two magazines from the box, along with two envelopes addressed to Grandma. An idea popped into her head.

As she entered the house she slipped part of the mail into her book and walked to Grandpa's desk. She laid the magazines on the desk and plopped into the recliner with her book.

"Nothing for me?" Grandma asked in a disappointed voice. Jeneva laughed and pulled the envelopes from her book. She

"Do I have a granddaughter who will get the mail for me?"

carried them to Grandma. "I was going to see if you would miss them. These two say 'Myrtle Petre.'" She dropped them onto Grandma's lap.

Brandon was sitting on the couch beside Grandma. She was reading *Rusty and Ryan* to him. When Grandma got to the bottom of the page she would say, "Turn," and Brandon would turn the page. Grandma's hands were weak, so if her grandchildren wanted her to read to them they had to help by holding the book and turning the pages.

Grandma stopped reading and fumbled to open her cards.

"I can open them," Brandon offered. He laid down the book and tore the envelopes open. He pulled the cards out and unfolded the letters for Grandma. Then he turned pages in the book and looked at pictures while Grandma read her mail.

When she was finished she said, "Thank you, Brandon, for opening my mail. I have to depend on others for so many things. Grandpa usually opens my mail."

"You're welcome. Maybe it was pay for you reading to me." Brandon grinned up at Grandma.

That evening Mama told Daddy how the children had helped that day. "I'm sure Grandma wishes she could do more by herself, but she doesn't complain much."

"I can't remember what is wrong with Grandma," Betty said. "Why don't her legs work?"

"Grandma has a disease called multiple sclerosis, or MS," Mama explained. "It makes her nerves and muscles weak."

Betty thought a little. "I wish the doctor could cut her open and take the disease out like he took out her kidney stones. Then he could sew her back shut and she could walk."

Mama patted Betty's head. "That isn't possible, dear. But when Grandma gets to heaven, God will give her a new body and it won't have any disease in it. Her new legs will be strong and healthy."

"Grandma will be happy in heaven," Jeneva added.

"Yes," Mama agreed. "Heaven will be wonderful. No sickness, death, pain, or tears; it is hard to imagine. No one will be cold or hungry, and no one will get old."

Brandon joined the conversation. "Maybe we will see Grandma walking in heaven. And we will see Uncle Ez. He is already there. He knows what heaven is like."

"I don't know how everything will be when we get to heaven," Mama said. "We cannot begin to imagine what God has prepared for those who love Him."

"The most important thing for us is to live godly lives so we are ready to go to heaven any time God calls for us," Daddy said.

That night the moon rose slowly and cast a silver glow over the Yoder family's house. Inside, the family slept safe and snug in their beds. At the other end of the road the same silvery moon shone down on Grandpa and Grandma's house where they, too, were sleeping soundly. The same God who made the moon was watching over them all. He would continue to give courage to Grandma Myrtle and strength to her helpers.

About the Author

Sylvia Yoder, wife of Don and mother of four, makes her home in the rolling land of southern Ohio. Born and raised in Tennessee, Sylvia has helped to care for her mother, Grandma Myrtle, for many years. Even at five years old, she supported her mother as she walked. Now Sylvia's own children have joined the care team.

Sylvia's favorite person to spend time with is her husband, Don, who builds storage buildings and sells swing sets and lawn furniture. Sylvia's favorite place to be is at home in her own little house, but she wants her children to know that the world is much larger than the state of Ohio. Her siblings are her best friends. She is passionate about helping others and enjoys working with her Basement Ministry friends doing projects for Christian Aid Ministries. She also enjoys animals, plants, interior design, and painting.

Sylvia and her family are members of Calvary Bible Fellowship. Her motto is: "The Bible has a verse for everything." Her goal is to live in obedience to the Word of God and to bring Him glory through her writing. Sylvia has written articles for *Inspiration*, a women's email publication; *Keepers at Home;* and a caregiver column in *Ladies' Journal.* She has participated in a writers' group for several years. *Grandma Myrtle and Her Helpers* is her first book.

You can contact Sylvia at sylviyoder@gmail.com or write to her in care of Christian Aid Ministries, P.O. Box 360, Berlin, Ohio 44610.

About Christian Aid Ministries

Christian Aid Ministries was founded in 1981 as a nonprofit, tax-exempt 501(c)(3) organization. Its primary purpose is to provide a trustworthy and efficient channel for Amish, Mennonite, and other conservative Anabaptist groups and individuals to minister to physical and spiritual needs around the world. This is in response to the command to ". . . do good unto all men, especially unto them who are of the household of faith" (Galatians 6:10).

Each year, CAM supporters provide 15–20 million pounds of food, clothing, medicines, seeds, Bibles, Bible story books, and other Christian literature for needy people. Most of the aid goes to orphans and Christian families. Supporters' funds also help to clean up and rebuild for natural disaster victims, put up Gospel billboards in the U.S., support several church-planting efforts, operate two medical clinics, and provide resources for needy families to make their own living. CAM's main purposes for providing aid are to help and encourage God's people and bring the Gospel to a lost and dying world.

CAM has staff, warehouses, and distribution networks in Romania, Moldova, Ukraine, Haiti, Nicaragua, Liberia, Israel, and Kenya. Aside from management, supervisory personnel, and bookkeeping operations, volunteers do most of the work at CAM locations. Each year, volunteers at our warehouses, field bases, Disaster Response Services projects, and other locations donate over 200,000 hours of work.

CAM's ultimate purpose is to glorify God and help enlarge His kingdom. ". . . whatsoever ye do, do all to the glory of God" (1 Corinthians 10:31)

The Way to God and Peace

We live in a world contaminated by sin. Sin is anything that goes against God's holy standards. When we do not follow the guidelines that God our Creator gave us, we are guilty of sin. Sin separates us from God, the source of life.

Since the time when the first man and woman, Adam and Eve, sinned in the Garden of Eden, sin has been universal. The Bible says that we all have "sinned and come short of the glory of God" (Romans 3:23). It also says that the natural consequence for that sin is eternal death, or punishment in an eternal hell: "Then when lust hath conceived, it bringeth forth sin: and sin, when it is finished, bringeth forth death" (James 1:15).

But we do not have to suffer eternal death in hell. God provided forgiveness for our sins through the death of His only Son, Jesus Christ. Because Jesus was perfect and without sin, He could die in our place. "For God so loved the world that he gave his only begotten Son, that whosoever believeth in him should not perish, but have everlasting life" (John 3:16).

A sacrifice is something given to benefit someone else. It costs the giver greatly. Jesus was God's sacrifice. Jesus' death takes away the penalty of sin for all those who accept this sacrifice and truly repent of their sins. To repent of sins means to be truly sorry for and turn away from the things we have done that have violated God's standards (Acts 2:38; 3:19).

Jesus died, but He did not remain dead. After three days, God's Spirit miraculously raised Him to life again. God's Spirit does something similar in us. When we receive Jesus as our sacrifice and repent of our sins, our hearts are changed. We become spiritually alive! We develop new desires and attitudes (2 Corinthians 5:17). We begin to make choices that please God (1 John 3:9). If we do fail and commit sins, we can ask God for forgiveness. "If we confess our sins, he is faithful and just to forgive us our sins, and to cleanse us from all unrighteousness" (1 John 1:9).

Once our hearts have been changed, we want to continue growing spiritually. We will be happy to let Jesus be the Master of our lives and will want to become more like Him. To do this, we must meditate on God's Word and commune with God in prayer. We will testify to others of this change by being baptized and sharing the good news of God's victory over sin and death. Fellowship with a faithful group of believers will strengthen our walk with God (1 John 1:7).